Secret Miracles
OF THERESE, JUDE AND BLAISE

JUANITA DE GUZMAN GUTIERREZ, BSED, MSED

To order additional copies of this book, contact:
Xlibris
1-888-795-4274
www.Xlibris.com
Orders@Xlibris.com

ISBN: Softcover   978-1-9845-8561-5
         EBook   978-1-9845-8562-2

Print information available on the last page

Rev. date: 06/29/2020

ABOUT THE BOOK

◇◇◇◇◇◇◇◇◇◇◇◇◇◇◇◇

I was about to choke on a big tilapia fish bone. The long bone was lodged opposite on either side of my throat. And each time, I breathe, the bone just got stuck inside my tonsils all the more! Then, I suddenly remembered to pray to Saint Blaise, and a great miracle happened!

I prayed for nine days to Saint Therese of Lisieux. Therese is famous for answering prayers with the signs of roses . And on the ninth day, a man was waiting at the bus stop with a bouquet of roses. He said it was for me!

I made a nine day prayer to Saint Jude. And I promised him that if my prayers will be granted that I will make him known. My prayers were granted and this is the reason why I am writing this book. And that is to spread the goodness of these three Ascended Masters, Galactic Stars, Avatars, we call saints. So you can all experience and live them in your reality, as well.
If not so, already.

And the powerful prayers or conversations or mantra to Therese, Blaise, and Jude are also in this book. Or, you also, can make your own words to acknowledge and communicate to them of your good intents for the good of mankind and of your own magnificent self.
Most of all.

Read the many more stories of miracles that I had personally experienced of these three fellow Gods and Goddesses, Kings and Queens, just as we are; known as Saints. And they are Saint Therese, Saint Jude, and Saint Blaise. It is because the God Source Energy is within inside of you and me. We are all Royalties as the Creator Source is home in our wonderful and compassionate hearts and brilliant and powerful minds. This is the reason why our heads is called Temple. And our hearts pulsate with love. As God Source is Love.

"God is Love. And all who live in Love abides in God. And God lives in him or her," as the scriptures state.

DECLARATION

In conformity with the decree of Pope Urban VIII, and the definitions of other Popes, the Author hereby declares that the statements contained in this book, are based solely on human authority for their trustworthiness.

—The Author

PREFACE

◇◇◇◇◇◇◇◇◇◇◇◇◇◇◇◇◇◇

There are so many miracles in our lives. Our very own lives are miracles in themselves. And our beautiful body is also a wonderful miracle. This is the reason why so many paintings and sculptures that bears the full body in its 'naked ' form, or in full regalia; so to speak, adorn so many museums and plaza in Europe.

I have seen these proofs during my many world travels since 1996 with my beloved mother. My beloved father had been working in the United States of America as a speed stenographer-typist in the airport and went to Heaven before Mom.

Our physical bodies are magnificent! A great and awesome work of art and science beyond compare. Only a Source Supreme Intelligence can fathom.

The extraterrestrials Beings led by Abraham as channeled by Esther Hicks, Kryon as channeled by Lee Carroll, and Bashar as channeled by Darryl Anka, had said that the Humans are the envy in the Universe because we have the God Source within. This is magnanimously brilliant, at its best!

Who can fathom the awesome magnificence of our brains, hearts, small and large intestine, eyes, skin, cells and so much more? They work in perfect harmony that we can never understand. A magnificent creation we indeed all are. ONE mankind in ONE Mother Earth.

And miracles of our fellow Gods and Goddesses, Galactic Stars such as Saint Therese, Saint Jude, and Saint Blaise are the three saints that so much touched my heart.

This is also in addition to Mother Mary, Our Lady of Guadalupe, that I featured in my book about her miraculous intercessions to me, in THE ROSE AND THE TILMA and the miracles of Anthony of Padua in another book that I wrote in, MISSING PEOPLE, ANIMALS, THINGS? GO TO ANTHONY, also published by Xlibris. As well as in my first book of miracles, "ADMIRABLE IS OUR GOD " published by Dorrance Publishing.

Read here the amazing and wonderful miracles of Saint Therese of Lisieux or Therese of the Child Jesus, Saint Jude, and Saint Blaise, that I have personally encountered.

DEDICATION

◇◇◇◇◇◇◇◇◇◇◇◇◇◇◇◇◇

This book is lovingly dedicated to my beautiful parents who have experienced the miracles of Saint Anthony of Padua as newlyweds during the Japanese Occupations of the Philippines in 1944. Mr. Jamito Javier Gutierrez and Mrs. Teodora Navarro de Guzman-Gutierrez, were two loving husbands and wife that were always devoted to each other and their children.

Loving dedications also goes to the Gutierrez children. All twelve in all. Four were taken to Heaven, Josefina, Joan, Thaddeus, and Thomas. The surviving children are Teodoro, Jacinta, Teodorico, Julita, Juanita, Jovita, Teodocio, and Jemena, and their respective families.

To all my acquaintances, former monastery sisters, former classmates, fellow schoolteachers, workers, and all Humanity; in general, and all Beings, in particular, this my book, is also lovingly dedicated.

To all the precious readers of this my book; loving dedications also go to you all, as well.

And to Source Creator, most of all, of which I credit my great energy of life, Our Lady of Guadalupe, and to Saint Anthony of Padua or Fernando Martins de Bulhoes, and all Ascended

Masters, Galactic Avatars, Extraterrestrials Benevolent Beings, this my book is most highly dedicated.

The Gutierrez Family. The Author's parents, the former Barangay Town Captain, Jamito Javier Gutierrez, and the first woman-councilor of the town, Teodora Navarro de Guzman-Gutierrez, with their eight surviving children from bottom left to right, are Teodoro, Jacinta, Teodorico, Julita, the Author's twin sister, Juanita, the Author, Jovita, Teodocio, and Jemena .

According to our beloved parents, the daughter's initial name-letters are taken from Dad. It symbolizes our father's love and commitment to defend and protect his girls. While the son's initial name-letter is taken from Mom so that the boys will protect and defend our mother.

Dad worked in the United States of America for more than twenty-five years as a stenographer at the airport of Wake Island, USA, to send all his children to university education. While our beloved mother stayed with us to care for us. Dad only went back home back to the Philippines once a month each year. God bless our parents for their love and commitment to us, their children.

ACKNOWLEDGEMENT

I am very grateful to my publisher, Xlibris, who have marvelously printed many of my books. And most especially the wonderful staff who are always there for me, beautiful and awesome. I thank you all very much.

DISCLAIMER

◇◇◇◇◇◇◇◇◇◇◇◇◇◇◇◇

Results will vary. Not all miracles happen to all people. Miracles do happen to different people; however much in variance they come. This book is written to inspire Humanity that we are, ourselves, great miracles! And also, that we have Galactic Helpers in times of need. And one of the many are Therese, Jude, and Blaise. There are many more of these miracles by our Extraterrestrials Guardian Angels in Miss Gutierrez' books and also by that of different writers.

The Author assumes no responsibility whatsoever before, during, and after reading this book. Take what resonates with you. Leave what does not. It's quite alright when it's not connecting with your wonderful self. Results will vary from person to person. It is not set in stone. The stories here do not intend to advice, diagnose, prevent, treat, nor cure any issues and are by no means a substitute for healthcare, medical, legal, nor financial advice. Always seek professional health, medical, legal, and financial assistance when needed.

TABLE OF CONTENTS

CHAPTER ONE—THE LIFE OF SAINT THERESE

◇◇◇◇◇◇◇◇◇◇◇◇◇◇◇◇

Saint Therese of the Child Jesus or of the Holy Face or the " Little Flower of Jesus, " is the youngest of the first parent, husband and wife Saints, as declared by Pope Francis I. These parents of Therese, Marie Azelle Guerin-Martin, and Louis Martin, did not even want to marry as a young man or woman. They did not know each other. And both have made it to themselves that they will not get married. At different times and place, as a young man and a young woman, each of them had seek entrance to a religious community . Louis Martin wanted to become a priest. And Marie wanted to become a nun. But each of them was not accepted.

You can just see the destiny of these two Human Beings already being predestined; in one way or another. It was said that when the two were walking for a stroll, and met each other not knowing each other yet, in the bridge where they were crossing, that Louis heard from his ear, " that is the woman you will marry." And Marie, on her part, also heard in her ear the same kind of message, " that is the man you will marry."

God Source will have their say. These two couples may not have been accepted in the convent or monastery they were applying to but all of their future four daughters will enter the religious life. And these two couples will be the first couple who were not martyrs to be declared saints by Pope Francis I in the twentieth century. And their youngest daughter. Therese will be declared a Saint at a young age and who entered the monastery at a tender age of thirteen.

Young Therese traveled with her father, Louis Martin to see Pope Leo XIII to beg him that she be accepted in the monastery. And all the Pope can say after he gave her the blessing is to wait for the signs of God.

Young Therese lost her mother, Marie Azelle Guerin-Martin, at a young age of four years old. And she climbed the chair facing their Altar at her home to touch the image of the Blessed Mother Mary to tell her, "now you are my mother."

One can see the destiny of this young child. One night, when young Therese as a five years old, was picked by her Dad from her baby sitter; the cute pie Therese had said to her Dad, " Dad, do you see my name written in the sky in the stars?" And her doting Dad agreed with her. The young Therese was already seeing visions as a very young child.

Therese was born in January 2, 1873 in Alencon in France. Her Feast Day is October 1. Therese went to Heaven on September 30, 1897 in Lisieux in France.
Her sisters are Genevieve, Leonie, and Pauline. Therese of the Child Jesus is declared as Doctor of the Church. Therese was born as Marie-Francoise Therese Martin. Another of Saint Therese' blood sister, Leonie, as of this writing in the Year 2020, is being considered for sainthood, as well. Leonie belongs in the Congregation of the Visitation of Holy Mary in France. Leonie Martin is also known as Sister Francoise Therese, VHM.

Therese was beatified in April 29, 1923 by Pope Pius XI. Therese was canonized as a Saint on May 17, 1925 by Pope Pius XI. The major shrine of Saint Therese is the Basilica of Saint Therese in Lisieux in France. Her other shrines are the National Shrine of Saint Therese in Darien, Illinois, USA. Another shrine of Saint Therese is in Royal Oak, Michigan m USA, the National Shrine of the Little Flower Basilica. Another shrine of Saint Therese is in the Philippines in Newport, Pasay City, named as the Shrine of Saint Therese of the Child Jesus.

CHAPTER TWO—Who Is Saint Blaise?

Saint Blaise is not as known as Saint Therese or Saint Jude . But Saint Blaise is also a very helpful friend-Saint. He was born in Sivas in Turkey. He went to Heaven in 316 Anno Domini, AD, Year of the Lord. His Feast Day is February 3.
As a side note, this date is my youngest sister's birthday, as well.

Saint Blaise came from Armenia from the land of Sebaste. He is known to be a doctor or a physician. He is also a martyr and was declared a Saint by the Eastern Church, Catholic Church, and Oriental Church.

Saint Blaise is known as the Patron Saint for those who are choking, those who are wool combers. Saint Blaise was born from a family of nobility. He is the patron saint of the throat ailments and those whose trade or job is a wool comber or those who shears the wool of a sheep.

This is the blessing-prayer attributed to Saint Blaise as the Patron of the throat:
"Through the intercession of Saint Blaise, Bishop and Martyr, May God deliver you from every disease of the throat and from every other illness."

As the above prayer is said to each individual, the two candles in the shape of a cross are placed in the neck or throat of the person. As a very devoted churchgoer, going to church twice a day, I am always the first in line after the Mass to receive the blessing-prayers of Saint Blaise from a priest . And I am always very relieved after these prayers.

I said that it is twice a day that I go to church because, before I go to school to work as I am a New York City School Teacher here in the USA, I attend the six o'clock morning Mass. And then after school, at four o'clock, I will go to another Mass in another church.

To go back to the story of Saint Blaise, it was said that during the time of Emperor Agricolaus, Cappadocia's governor, Saint Blaise was apprehended and was forced to worship pagan deities. When Saint Blaise refused, he was first beaten, then hung in a tree, and finally, was beheaded.

Saint Blaise is also famous in taming the animals. The wild animals listen to him. And this is true. As I have written in my book entitled, "SAVE THE WHALES, DOLPHINS, AND ALL SEA CREATURES ", where I have stated in my book that animals can talk to Humans and they do love us. And my fellow New York City School Teacher, Dianne Robbins, a clairvoyant has a daily communications with the Nature Kingdom Beings. Dianne Robbins has highly endorsed my four books, HUG A TREE, SMILE CRYSTAL PEOPLE LOVE YOU, UNICORNS MAKE US FLY HOBBITS SAY LIFE IS A PLAY, and my fourth book, SAVE THE WHALES DOLPHINS AND ALL SEA CREATURES. These my four books along with my other books are published by Xlibris and are available in all online stores worldwide.

It was said that when Saint Blaise was being led to his execution, a woman approached the Bishop and beg him to help her son who was choking with a fish bone. After the prayers of Saint Blaise, the boy began to throw up or cough the fish bone out safely. That is amazing! And I will say that it is amazing as I will relate in this my book in another chapter here how I was assisted by Saint Blaise as soon as I said the short prayers, mantra, or conversation to him.

During the incarceration of Saint Blaise, a woman came to the cave where Saint Blaise was incarcerated to give him two candles . The woman said he can use the two candles to light in his dark dungeon he was placed in as a prisoner. And this was in thanksgiving to him because Saint Blaise helped her in finding her lost pig. At the command of Saint Blaise. the fox brought back the pig unharmed.

Such a great Saint is Saint Blaise!

CHAPTER THREE—Saint Jude Thaddeus Biography

Saint Jude of Thaddeus is known as the Saint of the Impossible, Desperate, Hopeless, and Lost Cases. Why is he known as such? Let us see his biography. It was said that Jude was born in the First Century, Anno Domini, AD.

Jude of Thaddeus is the son of Mary of Cleophas who is the sister of the Blessed Lady Mary. Mary of Cleophas is the wife of Alpheus. Jude of Thaddeus is the writer of the Epistle of Saint Jude.

Jude is one of the Twelve Apostles. And he is a vegetarian or vegan. Vegan means people who are only eating vegetables.

Jude is always shown with the image of Jesus or Yeshua Ben Joseph in his chest or hand. Jude is also shown in pictures as having a flame in his head.

It was said that God had asked Saint Bridget of Sweden and Saint Bernard in a vision to let them know that Jude is the Patron of the Impossible. And that this declaration of God is to be accepted by them and the whole of mankind.

So now you know why Jude of Thaddeus is known as the Saint of the Impossible, Desperate, Hopeless Cases. It is God who had destined it. And the Feast of Saint Jude Thaddeus is in October 28.

There is also a hospital named after Jude Thaddeus. It is the Saint Jude's Research Hospital in Tennessee, USA.

CHAPTER FOUR—My Miraculous Experience With Saint Therese Of The Child Jesus And Holy Face

It is said that when one makes a prayer novena of nine days or twenty-four days to Saint Therese of the Child Jesus that one way you will know that she has answered your prayers favorably is when you receive roses before or close to the conclusion of your novena of nine days prayers or twenty-four days devotional prayers.

My personal miracles with Saint Therese of the Child Jesus took place as I was teaching in the New York City Public Schools here in the USA where I am.

The first one was when I was riding in the New York City Bus. As a New York City School Teacher, I get a discount annually in transportation passes. To take advantage of the discount, I purchase a whole year worth of subways rides that can be used in all public transportation around New York City, USA. So I always take the bus to work. Except when I have to go to Manhattan, then, I take the subway.

As I am sitting in the bus going to school for my teaching job and going back home, I always read my novena booklet that has all the saints' prayers and novenas. The word "novena" is a Latin word that means "nine days."

I would be reading this booklet the moment I got inside the bus all the way to when I reached the bus stop. And then after thirty minutes of traffic, my bus stopped to the same place I am getting off. As I was walking towards the door of the bus, I saw in the bus window a man carrying a bouquet of fresh red rose flowers. And I thought to myself he might be selling roses at this bus stop and he is going to hassle the passengers getting off to buy from him. And I also thought, that he might not be selling at all and might just be catching the bus for his work as a delivery person.

And then, I received the shock of my life! As I was still getting down the stairs of the bus, the man handed to me the bouquet of roses and walked away very quickly! And I did not have time to say anything! As a I walked to my school carrying the beautiful bouquet of red roses, I tried to control my tears.

When I reached my school, my principal asked me who that lucky person was who gave me the beautiful bouquet of flowers! She thought an admiring man just gave them to me.

The bouquet of roses were the proof that Saint Therese had heard my prayers and the concern that I have placed in her hand was instantly solved.

The second instance that I received the roses was when I made another novena or nine days of prayers and/or twenty-four days of prayers. I had met another obstacle and I asked Saint Therese to get me out of that situation.

So during the conclusion of my prayers I decided after my schoolteaching job to go to Manhattan. I attended a prayer mass celebration in honor of Saint Therese. After the Mass prayers, all the devotees were told that if they would like to join the procession, they should descend in the south door of the church.

So I started to walk down the aisle towards the south church door. There were so many people who attended the prayers celebration, so the line going down the stairs was slow. And then, when it was my turn to descend the steps, a man handed me a rose! Complete with its stem as if just newly plucked from the rose bushes! That was the first time that it happened when I attended a Mass prayers celebration in that church!

Again, I was so very deeply moved by the benevolence of Saint Therese. And I remember the famous line of Saint Therese, " I will make showers of roses fall from Heaven to those who asked for my intercession....."

Truly, in that procession as I was holding the rose, I again controlled my tears and I kept, in my mind, thanking Saint Therese endlessly.

Saint Therese really does listen to whoever is asking her favor.

And so, my book attests to this and my gratefulness to Saint Therese knows no bounds.

This is the reason why I have planned to write this book to show my great appreciation to Saint Therese and the other two saints in this my book. The other miracles that I have received from the other Ascended Masters are contained in my other published book, "ADMIRABLE IS OUR GOD."

CHAPTER FIVE—Saint Blaise, The Patron Of The Throat, His Awesome Intercession To Save Me

Each February 3 in church, I always come to the Holy Mass prayer celebrations to receive the blessings of Saint Blaise. The priest will tell us, parishioners, the wonderful miracle of Saint Blaise. After the homily or preaching of God's words, all of us, parishioners, will lined up in the aisle, and the priest will put the two candles in our throat near our necks and utter the prayers to Saint Blaise.

As I have also researched about the wonders of Saint Blaise on saving a boy that was choked by a fish bone; this was etched in my mind. And I thought to my self that it was so kind of Saint Blaise to have healed the boy choking from a fish bone.

And so I said to myself that Saint Blaise will always help anyone who will be choking with a fish bone.

Little did I know that one day, Saint Blaise powers of intercession will be put to the test!

I was very happy cooking my dinner. I cooked some rice and had a fish stew of tilapia fish. So after I have put everything in my plate, a scoop of rice and a bowl of the fish stew, I started eating. It taste so very good, I thought.

I did not know that a huge fish bone was lodged in my rice that when I began to swallow the rice, it was too late to get the big fish bone out from my throat. I kept in swallowing but the more the fish bone got stuck in my throat!

I tried to calm myself. I was alone and live alone in my New York City Apartment, USA. And I do not want fear to overtake me. But my throat is getting painful with that big fish bone lodged in my tonsil . And I remembered Saint Blaise. And in my mind, almost in tears, I said to myself, " Saint Blaise, this is your time to help me. Please, Saint Blaise, remove this fish bone out of my throat. I do not know how but only you can do it."

And as soon as I said those words, I began to throw up. It was as if someone had induced my mouth to vomit. And in that instant, a big fish bone got out of my mouth and into my plate!

I was overjoyed and in tears of thanksgiving to Saint Blaise! And I said to Saint Blaise as if he was in front of me, " Saint Blaise, thank you very much from the bottom of my heart forever. And in thanksgiving for this great assistance, I will make you known and your power of intercession to those who are in need."

And so, when I went back to school the next morning where I am a school teacher, I told my students and fellow teachers about the greatness of Saint Blaise and his powerful miracles in helping me take out the fish bone from my throat. And the most important and highlight of my story is that Saint Blaise is the one to call in distress when in need of help of any problems especially in the throat.

And I did not know that someday I will be writing books. This is now my fifteenth book, with Source Energy's help to be published. Therefore, my writing of books will triple the chance of me propagating the goodness of Saint Blaise and his mission in aiding those who need help especially in the assistance with throats.

Thank you so very much, Saint Blaise, always and forever. You are a very kind, quick-to-help, Ascended Master Saint, to those who invoke your name. Pray for us. And so it is.

CHAPTER SIX—MY WONDERFUL EXPERIENCE WITH SAINT JUDE, THE PATRON OF IMPOSSIBLE CASES

I have been a new school teacher in the public schools and each afternoon after school and even on Sundays after the Holy Mass prayer celebrations, I will always go to the shrine of Saint Jude . And I will always light a candle in front of the huge, almost human size bust of Saint Jude. And as I light the candle and after placing my donations, I will say in my mind what my intentions were to him.

And I always say after saying my petitions that if my petition is granted that I will let him be known all over the world. I said to Saint Jude, in my mind, that as a promise, I will let the world know of his power of intercession and of his good deeds in granting what the devotee of him is asking.

After a month of lighting candles to the shrine of Saint Jude, my petitions had been answered and granted!

And I was so ecstatically overjoyed!

So, I started buying novena cards that contain powerful prayers to Saint Jude. And I will give them for free to anyone who would accept it. Then, I thought of mailing them to people. I bought from a mailing company a list of names. Sometimes, a few of the mails come back. The mailing company would say that the reason of returned mails is maybe because the person have moved to another place.

And I will do this mailings for years. And sometimes, when a I ran out of money in purchasing stamps, I will just leave the prayer cards to Saint Jude in church lobbies, public libraries, banks, stores, and other places where people mostly congregate.

And I am so happy that I am able to write a book and publish this to be read and be available worldwide over the Internet. Not in my wildest dreams that I will be writing and publishing many books. Although, I said to myself that it would be a wonderful blessing to be able to see my name in the front cover of my book that I wrote. But I did not think that it would be possible so very quickly.

And now; through the help of Saint Jude Thaddeus, and the other saints here with the Source Energy God, this book of mine, is already my fifteenth book that I have written and published. And possibly, more with the manifestation blessing of Source Energy God within me and us all.

And so it is true that Saint Jude Thaddeus is the Saint of the Impossible Cases and Of Things Almost Despaired Of. It is because what I have asked of him was I thought very impossible to have taken place. And Saint Jude made it possible.

I know that with the blessing of the God Source Energy within me, and all the Galactic Family of Light, the Pleidians, Agarthan, of which I belong, who have always assisted me, with the intercession of Saint Jude Thaddeus, Saint Therese of Lisieux of the Little Child Jesus, and Saint Blaise, that this my book in their honors is published.

So that all may know that we have Heavenly helpers who care about us if we only ask for their assistance. And to believe that what we are asking will be realized according to God's plan.

EPILOGUE

Miracles happen daily the moment each child is born. Every living Being has the Divine Source Energy within our hearts, minds, and feelings. These saints and/or Ascended Masters are here to assist us when the journey gets a little tougher to handle. And these three Avatars Or Ascended Masters by the name of Saint Blaise, Saint Jude, and Saint Therese have etched their marks in my whole being that cannot be erased.

This beautiful book is a witness of their love to me and my love to them.

All of you, my dear Readers, and fellow Royals, Gods, Goddesses, Kings, and Queens are capable of tapping these three wonderful fellow Masters of ours when we need their help.

And may Saint Therese, Saint Jude, and Saint Blaise pray for us and bless us always with well-being, best of health, safety, peace, prosperity of all good, and joy always and forever.

And so it is.

BOOKS WRITTEN BY THE AUTHOR, JUANITA DE GUZMAN GUTIERREZ, BSED, MSED.

BOOKS BY THE AUTHOR now available in all bookstores worldwide,
online at Xlibris, Amazon, eBay, Amazon Author Central Page

1. SPEAK TAGALOG published by outskirtspress in Colorado, USA.

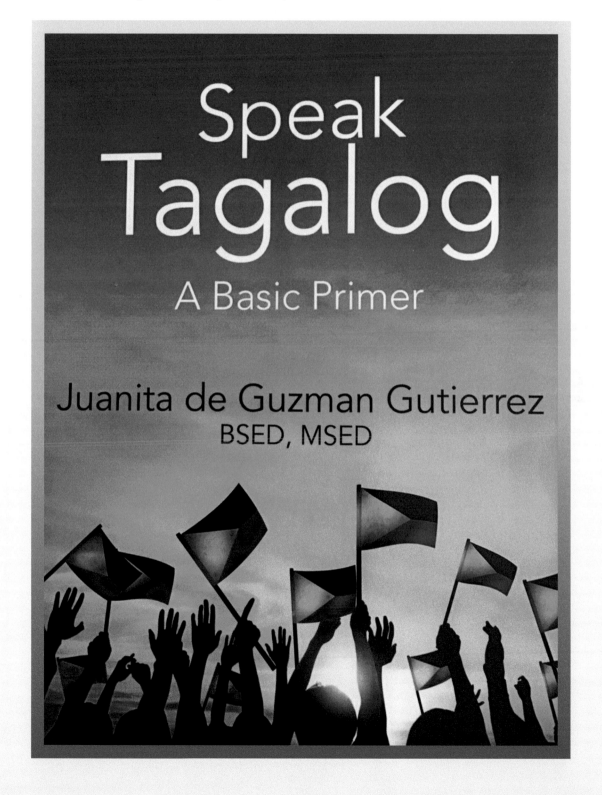

2. ADMIRABLE IS OUR GOD published by Dorrance Publication, Pittsburgh, PA, USA.

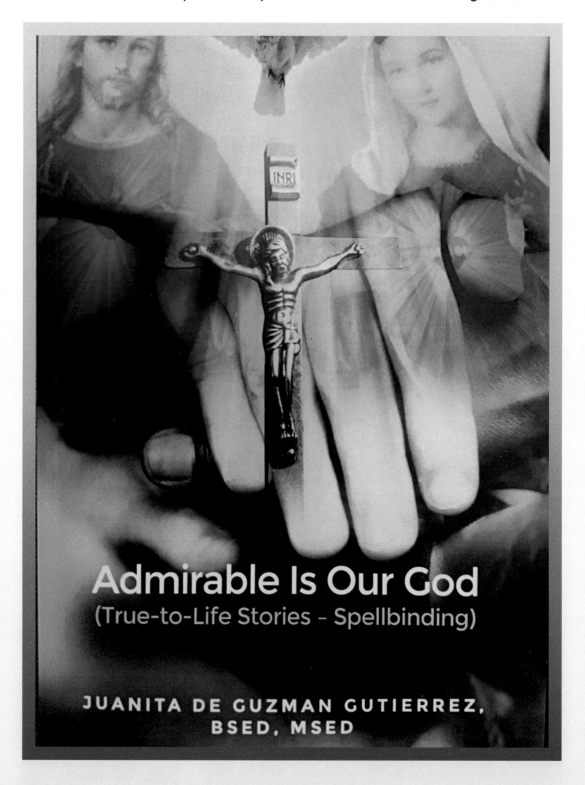

3. CHRIST-LIKE MOM AND DAD published by Xlibris, Bloomington, Indiana, USA.

4. HOW TO DISCERN IF GOD CALLS YOU TO MONASTERY LIFE published by AuthorHouse, Bloomington, Indiana, USA.

5. HUG A TREE published by Xlibris, Bloomington, Indiana, USA.

6. SAVE THE WHALES, DOLPHINS AND ALL SEA CREATURES published byXlibris, Bloomington, Indiana, USA.

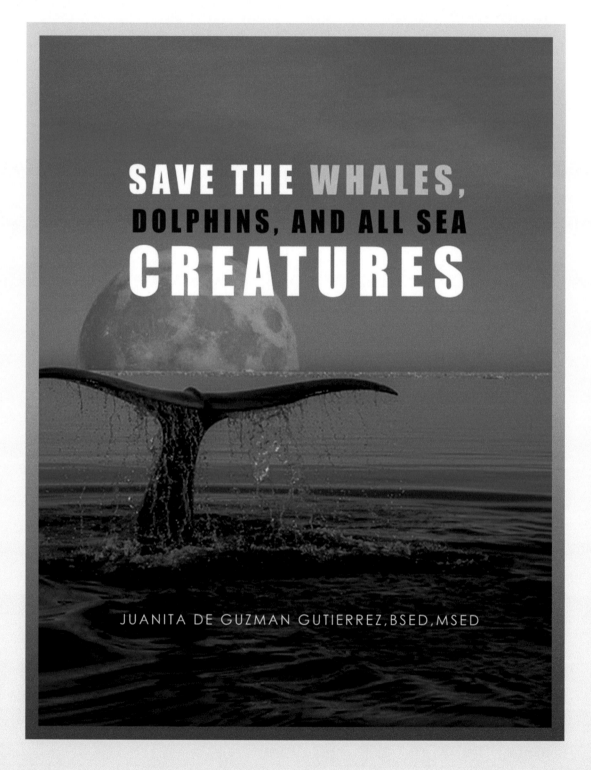

7. MOM-IN-CHEF, NANAY NENE TEODORA OF PHILIPPINES CUISINE COOKBOOK RECIPES, published by Xlibris, Bloomington, Indiana, USA.

8. BELOVED JESUS MARRIED TO MARY, A LOVE REVOLUTION, published by Xlibris, Bloomington, Indiana, USA.

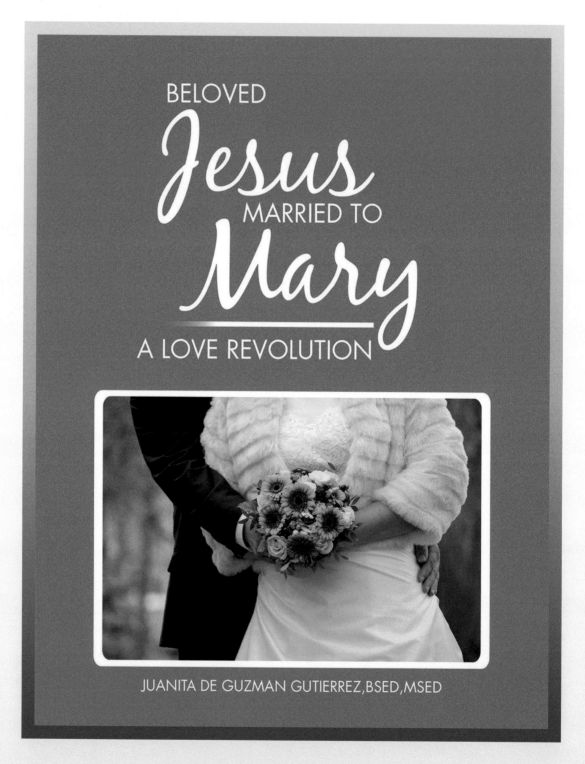

9. HOW TO BE HAPPY, REALLY AND TRULY, published by Xlibris, Bloomington, Indiana, USA.

10. ABANDON RACISM AND WELCOME OUR FELLOW EXTRATERRESTRIALS, published by Xlibris, Bloomington, Indiana, USA.

11. SMILE, CRYSTAL PEOPLE LOVE YOU, published by Xlibris, Bloomington, Indiana, USA.

12. UNICORNS MAKE US FLY, HOBBITS SAY LIFE IS A PLAY, published by Xlibris, Bloomington, Indiana, USA.

13. THE ROSE AND THE TILMA, published by Xlibris, Bloomington, Indiana, USA.

14. MISSING PEOPLE, ANIMALS, THINGS? GO TO ANTHONY, published by Xlibris, Bloomington, Indiana, USA.

15. SECRET MIRACLES OF THERESE, JUDE AND BLAISE, published by Xlibris, Bloomington, Indiana, USA.

ABOUT THE AUTHOR

◇◇◇◇◇◇◇◇◇◇◇◇◇◇◇◇

Juanita de Guzman Gutierrez graduated with the degree of Master of Science in Education from Fordham University in New York City, USA. Miss Gutierrez graduated with her degree of Bachelor of Science in Education from the University of the East, Manila, Philippines.

Miss Gutierrez had been a school teacher for more than thirty-three years. Ten years in the Public Schools of Quezon at the school where her beloved mother was the first woman ever elected public official, unanimously and a topnotcher, and had helped founded as the only and first public high school in her hometown. This was the school where Miss Gutierrez had first taught as a fresh graduate from her university education. Her beloved father was twice elected Town Captain or Mayor who approved the school budget. This was after his father's retirement as a stenographer-typist in the USA Airport.

In the City Schools of Manila, in the Philippines, Miss Gutierrez was a school paper adviser and Journalism teacher that won for her several awards and her student-writers winning in writing contests.

Miss Juanita de Guzman Gutierrez was hired to teach in the Archdiocese of New York Catholic Schools, USA, for five years.

Miss Gutierrez then transferred to teach in the Public Schools of the City of New York, New York, USA. She was the speaker and trainer of teachers during Teachers Institutes and seminars-workshops.

She entered for three years and three months inside the monastery in Virginia, USA, to discern a religious vocation. It was not God's Holy will for her to become a nun. Miss Gutierrez had to be let go of her superior to be the primary caregiver of her beloved mother.

Miss Gutierrez had traveled to Europe with her beloved mother in 1996 in London, England, Paris in France, Switzerland, Belgium, The Netherlands, Germany, Holland.

In 2014, Miss Gutierrez traveled to The Holy Lands of Israel, Palestine, Jericho, Golgotha, Bethlehem, Capernaum, Dead Sea, Masada Mountains, and other Sacred sites.

Then in 2015, Miss Gutierrez went on a Pilgrimage Tour to Rome in Italy, Lourdes in France, Fatima in Portugal, Assisi in Italy, Madrid and Zaragoza in Spain.

In Mexico in 2018, Miss Juanita de Guzman Gutierrez traveled to see the famous Living Painting of Our Lady of Guadalupe. Miss Gutierrez wrote a book, "THE ROSE AND THE TILMA", that catalogued the many miracles she had encountered before, during, and after her tour to Mexico.

Miss Gutierrez had written fourteen books when she started writing in 2014 when she left the monastery to take care of her beloved mother. Her beautiful and beloved mother went to the Heavenly Realms in 2015.

Miss Gutierrez worked as a cashier of a nonprofit organization for one year and three months.

The author, Miss Gutierrez, had retired early young from public school teaching in the City Schools of New York, USA in December of 2010 to enter the monastery in Richmond Virginia to discern the call to the religious life.

In 2014, she left the monastery to be the primary caregiver of her beloved mother.

Miss Gutierrez, the Author, now devote her time to relaxing, travels, and writings.

The Author in New York City, USA, where she is a New York City School Teacher . She is shown here at Niagara Falls top deck as she visited the wonders of the world very often.

The Author on the mountain top of the Masada Mountains in Israel and Palestine. The mountain ranges could only be reached by a skyway cable car provided to all tourists-travelers. Photo taken during Miss Gutierrez' Pilgrimage Tour To The Holy Lands.

The Author wading in the waters of the Jordan River where Yeshua or Jesus was baptized. Photo taken during Miss Gutierrez' Tour To The Holy Lands comprising Israel, Palestine, Bethlehem, Jericho, Capernaum, Bethsaida, Golgotha, and all places where Yeshua Ben Joseph, otherwise known as Jesus, had walked upon.

The Author and her beloved mother, Mrs. Teodora Gutierrez, at Paris in France during their European World Tour comprising seven countries of London in Great Britain, Switzerland, Germany, The Netherlands, Belgium, and Holland. Photo taken behind the Arch of Triumph where the Emperor Napoleon Bonaparte of France entered after winning the Battle of Austerlitz. The Arch de Triumphe extends to the Louvre, the largest museum in the world, where Miss Gutierrez and her beloved mother also visited along with the accompanying tourist group. The two are also wearing a souvenir tee shirt showing the Eiffel Tower, where they also have seen personally, and these shirts bought in Paris, France. The Author's father, Town Leader, Mr. Jamito Gutierrez, worked as a stenographer-fast typist at the airport in the USA for more than twenty-five years; and had already gone to Heaven previously.

Printed in the United States
By Bookmasters